GRACE

GRACE

⚞ A PLAY ⚟

CRAIG WRIGHT

NORTHWESTERN UNIVERSITY PRESS

EVANSTON, ILLINOIS

Northwestern University Press
www.nupress.northwestern.edu

The lines of verse on page 54 are from Stéphane Mallarmé's poem "Apparition" (1863); the English translation is by Roger Fry from *Poems* (London: Chatto & Windus, 1936).

Printed in the United States of America

10 9 8 7 6 5 4 3 2 1

ISBN 978-0-8101-2899-6

Library of Congress Cataloging-in-Publication data are available from the Library of Congress.

∞ The paper used in this publication meets the minimum requirements of the American National Standard for Information Sciences—Permanence of Paper for Printed Library Materials, ANSI Z39.48-1992.

For Rob Wething

CONTENTS

PRODUCTION HISTORY

Grace was originally commissioned and produced by Woolly Mammoth Theatre Company at the Warehouse Theater in Washington, D.C., on October 25, 2004. It was directed by Michael John Garcés; the set design was by James Kronzer; the lighting design was by Lisa L. Ogonowski; the costume design was by Debra Kim Sivigny; the sound design was by Neil McFadden; the original music was by Cristian Amigo; and the production stage manager was Taryn Colberg. The cast was as follows:

Steve . . . . David Fendig
Sara . . . . Jennifer Mendenhall
Sam . . . . Paul Morella
Karl . . . . Michael Willis

Grace was produced by Northlight Theatre in Chicago on February 1, 2006. It was directed by Dexter Bullard; the set design was by Jack Magaw; the lighting design was by Robert Christen; the costume design was by Tiffany Bullard; the sound design was by Joseph Fosco; and the production stage manager was Ellen Hay. The cast was as follows:

Steve . . . . Steve Key
Sara . . . . Chaon Cross
Sam . . . . Michael Shannon
Karl . . . . Mike Nussbaum

Grace was produced on Broadway by Debbie Bisno, Fox Theatricals, Jed Bernstein, and Paula Wagner in New York City at the Cort Theatre, opening on October 4, 2013. It was directed by Dexter Bullard; the set design was by Beowulf Boritt; the lighting design was by David Weiner; the costume design was by Tif Bullard; the sound design was by Darron L. West; and the production stage manager was James Harker. The cast was as follows:

Steve . . . . Paul Rudd
Sara . . . . Kate Arrington
Sam . . . . Michael Shannon
Karl . . . . Edward Asner

GRACE

CHARACTERS

Steve, *male, thirties*

Sara, *female, thirties*

Sam, *male, thirties*

Karl, *male, seventies*

SETTING

The play takes place in two identical generic apartments on the Florida shore. There is only one set for both apartments, however, and we are in both of them all of the time. The time is the present.

SCENE 1

[*A gunshot rings out and lights rise on two dead bodies—one woman and one man—lying on the floor of a condominium on the Florida shore. Standing with a gun to his head is* STEVE. *Time is moving backward. He takes the gun from his head. He takes a few steps, aims the pistol at the dead woman—*SARA*—and shoots. She stands, driven upright like a lightning bolt. She screams. He turns and aims at the dead man—*SAM*—who shoots upward into a standing position as well.* STEVE *holds the gun there, aimed at* SAM.]

SAM: Don't. Please. Don't.

[STEVE *cocks the gun.*]

SARA: We can't.

STEVE: I want to go back. Remember the little monkeys? I want to go back, Sara!

SARA: Please, Steve, just tell me what you want—

STEVE: It feels like it does! It feels like it does, though, doesn't it?

SARA: It doesn't have to!

STEVE: *Just tell me this is how it ends up!!*

SARA: Don't!

[STEVE *lowers the gun.*]

STEVE: It felt like the most perfection and beauty I'd ever felt in my life, and this is how it ends up? I reorganized my entire life around this "universal love" that I thought I saw, that I thought I felt. I changed everything. And so I did what any poor, stupid, helpless human being would do. "Universal love." I talked to the stars and they talked back and something shot through me, it did, down through the top of my head like an upside-down fountain and I was filled for the first time with a sense of love. I would give anything, anything, to forget they did, but I can't. I spoke to them like you would to a person, and they talked back. Because some people had told me something, I went outside and looked up at the stars. Because a lot of people had, what, told me something? The stars? One night I went out under the stars. God.

SCENE 2

[*The time is three months earlier.* SAM's *MacBook Pro is open on the coffee table. Amy Grant's pop-gospel classic "In a Little While" is playing loudly on a CD boom box. Otherwise, no one's on the set. We hear keys in the door, and* STEVE *enters in a suit and tie, pleased as punch, bearing a grocery bag and a briefcase.*]

STEVE: Hey!

[SARA *enters from the bedroom.*]

SARA: Hi.

[STEVE *sets the grocery bag down.*]

STEVE: Guess what?

SARA: What?

STEVE: *Guess.*

SARA [*not enjoying guessing and not ever imagining this is it*]: You got the call.

STEVE: I got the call.

[*Beat.*]

SARA [*shocked and happy*]: No WAY—Steve!

STEVE: I know!

SARA: You got the CALL!

STEVE: I KNOW! They're issuing the bonds in Zurich right now!

SARA: Praise God!

STEVE: I know, I was praying the whole way home in the car, Sara, I was speaking in tongues and people were looking at me, like, "What's up with him?"

SARA: This is so amazing!

STEVE: Sara, you don't even *know*!

[STEVE *and* SARA *embrace.*]

It's amazing, it's crazy, it's the LORD, can I turn the music off a second?

SARA: Sure, of course—

STEVE: Because I wanna tell you all about it.

SARA: I know, please, turn it off, I want to hear!

[*Just as* STEVE *turns off the stereo,* SAM *enters from the kitchen. His face is half covered in bandages.* SAM *walks painfully with a drugstore cane and has one arm in a sling.* SAM *doesn't notice* STEVE *and* SARA. *They are in two different apartments.*]

SAM [*to himself*]: Thank you, fucking Jesus.

SARA: We should pray first.

STEVE [*thrown slightly off course but not showing it*]: Totally.

[STEVE *and* SARA *take each other's hands, bow their heads: a team.* SAM, *meanwhile, sits at the laptop and starts working frustratedly.*]

STEVE: Dear Lord, we just come before You now to thank You for bringing us this amazing opportunity . . .

SARA: Praise You, Lord . . .

STEVE: For giving us the courage to come down here to Florida all the way from Minnesota . . . for giving us the courage as a couple to follow You *wherever* You lead us in life, and for, just, blessing us with all Your bounty . . .

SARA: Yes, Lord . . .

STEVE: And we just want to ask You to please help us continue, Lord, even at times like this, when You're showering us with so many blessings, help us to keep being faithful followers of You . . .

SARA: Even more faithful . . .

STEVE: Yes, even more faithful, and help us keep our eyes on You, Lord, through all of it, and on Your Son, Jesus Christ, upon whom we depend . . .

SARA: Completely . . .

STEVE: Yes, upon whom we depend *completely*, and we just come before You now and ask You to just keep holding us, Lord. Keep carrying us forward, Lord, always forward, deeper and deeper into Your grace. Amen.

[STEVE *opens his eyes—he's done. But* SARA's *eyes are still closed.* STEVE *waits, loving her.* SARA *smiles, feeling a genuine deep peace.*]

SARA: Amen.

[SARA *opens her eyes.*]

Thank you.

[STEVE *and* SARA *kiss simply and quickly. Then,* SARA *continues like the best mom ever—*]

OK, so what happened? Tell me!

STEVE: Well, I got a call, like, last thing, last minute, just like these things always happen, just as I'm walking out the door, I get this call from Gary Oliver, he said Mr. Himmelman loves the location, he's approved the purchase, it's all systems go, they're gonna wire us the money from Zurich tomorrow morning!

SARA: Steve, that's so amazing! I'm so happy for you!

STEVE: I know, but do you know what it means?

SARA: We can have a baby?

STEVE: Yes, we can have a baby, but what it means is, Sara, is the principles work!

[SARA *steps away from* STEVE, *headed to get something.*]

I mean, do you know what I can do now that I know this, REALLY, that the Lord really works this way? What I can achieve in the hotel industry?

SARA [*as if this is enough*]: Whatever the Lord wants you to achieve!

STEVE [*as if that was not quite enough*]: Yeah, whatever we want to!

[SARA *grabs a Pottery Barn catalog and sits on the sofa.*]

SARA: Come here.

STEVE: Why?

SARA: I wanna show you something.

STEVE: Wait a second, just let me tell you one more thing.

SARA [*a micro-stutter of intention*]: I'm, uh, OK.

[SARA *keeps the catalog in her lap.*]

STEVE: I figured out the name.

SARA: For the hotel?

STEVE: For the whole CHAIN.

SARA: Tell me.

STEVE: "Crossroads Inns . . ."?

SARA: I don't like that name.

STEVE: Why? It's the perfect name for a chain of gospel hotels! "Crossroads Inns!"

SARA: I don't know . . .

STEVE: Sara—

SARA: "Crossroads Inns . . ."

STEVE: What?

SARA: There's just something hard to say about it—

STEVE: What's hard to say? "Crossroads Inns! Crossroads Inns?" What's hard?

SARA: In the middle there, "Crossroads Inns," it's "zins," it's weird—

STEVE: No it isn't—

SARA: And what do you call the ONE?

STEVE: What do you mean?

SARA: What do you call the ONE hotel—

STEVE: Which ONE hotel?

SARA: The one you're about to buy; when you're done with the renovation and you open the doors, is it gonna be the "Crossroads
INN"?

STEVE: I guess.

SARA: But the chain is called "Crossroads INNS . . ."? It's weird.

STEVE [*moving on*]: What about "The Upper Rooms"?

SARA: That feels sacrilegious—

STEVE [*only half as a joke*]: "The New RESTament"?

SARA [*smiling at the half-joke*]: Steve—

STEVE: What?

SARA: Would you sit down and look at this with me now, please?

STEVE: OK, but just for a second, I'm so pumped!

[STEVE *sits on the sofa arm beside* SARA *but doesn't pay attention.*]

What's up?

SARA: Look.

[SARA *shows* STEVE *the catalog.* KARL, *having entered from the kitchen,
has finished spraying in the living room and comes over to* SAM—KARL
speaks with a German accent and is ancient.]

KARL: S'okay if I go in the bedroom?

[SAM *nods.* KARL *exits.* STEVE's *not sure what to look at.*]

STEVE: What?

SARA [*pointing*]: There.

STEVE [*masking an essential weariness*]: Oh, *baby* stuff.

SARA: Yeah, for the baby's *room.*

STEVE: You're not pregnant right now, are ya?

SARA: No, it would be for when we *have* one, silly. It's all a whole big set.

STEVE: Looks great!

SARA: You see the pattern? On the bedding, the ruffle, the curtains . . . ?

STEVE: What are those things? [*After a closer look*] Little monkeys?

SARA: Yeah. I think they're so precious, don't you?

STEVE: Yeah, I think they're totally precious.

SARA: They're on sale right now.

STEVE: Great!

SARA: This whole catalog is discontinued lines . . .

STEVE: I think it's all great!

SARA: So even if we don't have a baby right now, we should just get the set—

STEVE: I agree.

SARA: Because I love those little monkeys! I just wanna *have* 'em, you know?

STEVE: I completely agree.

SARA: Yeah?

STEVE: Yeah, the minute the money comes through tomorrow morning, I'll throw some cash into our personal account, done.

[*After a long beat.*]

SARA: But—

STEVE: What?

SARA: They're discontinued lines.

STEVE: So they can't wait until tomorrow . . . ?

SARA: I don't know. It says supplies are limited—

STEVE: You think they send out a catalog with only one piece of everything left? So it's, like, a *race*?

SARA: I don't know, I just want to get 'em! That's all!

STEVE: Look, Sara, I promise, the minute the money comes tomorrow, we'll transfer some cash into our account and you can order it. OK?

SARA: But—

STEVE: Let's just do things in order. It's just one day. It's less than one day.

SARA: OK. But promise.

STEVE: I promise. We'll get the little monkeys tomorrow.

SARA: Thank you.

STEVE: Thank YOU.

[STEVE *and* SARA *kiss.* STEVE *pulls away from the kiss and goes to the kitchen to start unpacking the grocery bag.*]

Now, do you have plans for dinner, 'cause I got some big steaks.

SARA: Wait!

STEVE: What?

SARA: Don't take anything out.

STEVE: Why not?

SARA [*with a very light edge*]: Because the exterminator hasn't come, everything's put away, and I don't wanna get insecticide all over the food.

STEVE: Oh. OK.

[KARL *has come out of the bedroom with his sprayer and a work order in one hand.*]

KARL: If you'll sign this here, I'll skedaddle.

[SAM *signs the work order.* STEVE *steps out of the kitchen.*]

STEVE: So let's just go out to dinner.

SARA: No, we can't.

STEVE: Why not?

SARA: Because I have to wait to let him in . . .

[KARL *opens the front door and addresses* SAM.]

KARL [*dismally*]: Have a good one.

SARA: . . . anyway, we can't afford to go out.

[KARL *exits, closing the door behind him.*]

STEVE: Why can't we afford to go out?

SARA: Because we don't have the money.

STEVE: I told you, we're getting the money tomorrow morning from Zurich.

SARA: I know, but we don't have the money in Florida tonight.

STEVE: So we'll charge it.

SARA: So we can charge dinner but we can't charge the little monkeys . . . ?

[*There is a knock at the door.* STEVE *heads for the door.*]

STEVE: Dinner is not the little monkeys, Sara, dinner's dinner and the little monkeys are a thousand dollars' worth of monkey-covered stuff!

[STEVE *gets to the door.*]

DOG!

[*Beat.* STEVE *feels bad for having said that.*]

I'm sorry.

SARA: It's OK. I'm sorry, too. It's just—I've been here all day.

STEVE: I know. I'm sorry.

SARA: OK.

STEVE: OK.

[*Beat.* STEVE *opens the door. Standing there is* KARL.]

STEVE: Hi.

KARL: Hey.

STEVE: Come on in.

KARL: Sorry I'm late. S'been kind of a toughie.

STEVE: No problem.

[KARL *enters, sets down his sprayer, and prepares to spray.*]

KARL: You two wanna go outside while I do this?

STEVE: No, you just do your thing.

KARL: Okey dokey.

[KARL *starts spraying.* STEVE *gives* SARA *a look. She affirms.*]

STEVE: So what went wrong with your day?

KARL: Huh?

STEVE: You said you've had a tough day, I think, what happened?

KARL: Oh, boy, you name it. First, those tourists got shot on the free-
way . . .

STEVE: Oh, yeah. [*To* SARA] Did you hear about that?

SARA: No.

STEVE: A family was on their way to, uh, Orlando from the airport,
right?

KARL: Yah.

STEVE:—just landed, they were on their way to Disney World, of all
places, and some kids just pulled up alongside, shot the dad and the
children dead.

KARL: I was in traffic for three hours behind that nonsense.

STEVE: We should probably get a pistol for the car.

SARA: Are you kidding?

KARL: S'not a bad idea. S'a third time this month someone got popped.

STEVE [*to* SARA]: Third time, Sara.

KARL: And when the hurricanes come, there's always the looters, you know, you gotta keep them back at the perimeter, stand your ground.

STEVE: Stand your ground, Sara . . .

SARA: I don't want a gun in my life!

STEVE: I'm not asking you to decide!

SARA: I get that! Thanks!

[SAM *registers surprise and shouts at his computer.*]

SAM: Fuck!

STEVE: So what else, uh, happened with your day?

KARL: Oh, well, y'know, you name it—

SAM [*giving the computer the finger*]: Fuck you!

KARL:—my wife's very sick with cancer in her female parts . . .

SARA: I'm sorry.

KARL: S'okay, it's not your fault, but *she* calls me all day crying from the hospital, s'very sad, and then that neighbor of yours, next door, *whoo!*

STEVE: We haven't really gotten to know him yet—

SARA [*half-overlapping*]: Or even seen him, really—

KARL: Well, trust me, he's the icing on the cake!

STEVE: What'd he do?

KARL: Oh boy. S'a sad story. S'a sad, sad story.

[KARL *sprays as he talks. And* SAM, *meanwhile, gets up, stomps into the bedroom, and then returns with his camera.*]

This guy is some sort of, uh, computer genius for NASA, with the pretty girlfriend, the good looks, the whole nine yards, until one day, they go out driving in their Miata down the Highway One.

STEVE [*to* SARA]: That's a cute little car.

KARL: Yah, it's cute, but then a tanker truck full of orange juice pulls up alongside them and doesn't see them as he's moving over to turn onto the Tropicana access road, knocks the Miata over, and bam, kills the girl dead.

[SAM *uses a cord to plug the camera into his MacBook Pro.*]

SARA: Oh, no.

KARL: Yah, but wait. There's more. Then, flipped over like that, the car slides about a hundred feet on the shoulder, and as it's going along, schmear, it scrapes half the skin off the poor guy.

STEVE: How do you know all this?

KARL: Huh?

STEVE: Who told you what happened?

KARL: The girl in the office. She warn me before I go in, because all he does is sit there, you know . . . alone all the time, and he looks kinda bad. S'pretty sad.

STEVE [*to* SARA]: You should check in on him.

SARA: I will.

KARL [*to* STEVE]: S'okay if I go in the bedroom?

STEVE: Sure.

KARL [*to* SARA]: I always ask.

[KARL *exits into the bedroom.* STEVE *and* SARA *argue quietly.*]

SARA: I don't want a gun in my home.

STEVE: It would be in the car—

SARA: I don't care! I don't want a gun!

STEVE: This is not Minnesota, Sara. It's Florida! It's a little different!

SARA: If it's that different, maybe we shouldn't be here!

STEVE: Well, it's a little late for that, now that everything's working out!

[SARA *walks to the bedroom door and talks to* KARL.]

SARA: Sir?

KARL [*offstage*]: Yah?

SARA: What exactly are you spraying for?

KARL [*offstage*]: Huh?

SARA: What kind of bugs are you spraying for?

KARL [*offstage*]: Ohhh, palmetto bugs. Thrips. Couch crickets. You name it.

SARA: And are they really that dangerous?

STEVE: Sara, just let the man do his work.

SARA [*to* STEVE, *sotto voce*]: I hate that we're doing this.

STEVE [*sotto voce*]: Sara, we can't be living with bugs.

SARA [*while looking at* STEVE]: Is killing them really necessary?

[KARL *comes out of the bedroom.*]

KARL: Yah, it's pretty much recommended. You know, in these warmer climates, even when it seems like you're all alone, you know, the little guys are everywhere, waitin' in the wings. I saw a house yesterday—this s'a sad story—I saw a house yesterday where there were almost more termites in the house than could even hold the place together anymore.

STEVE: Dog.

KARL [*after a micro-beat for "Dog"*]: Yah. Every space where there was structure in the place was become filled with them. You couldn't see it. But you could feel it. There was a "vvmm" under the surface, a "vvvmmmmm."

STEVE: Dog.

KARL: Yah. The little guys had become the whole structure of the house. The whole house was alive . . . and breakin' up . . . at the same time. S'pretty sad.

[KARL *starts spraying again.*]

STEVE: So you're spraying for termites here too, I hope?

KARL: No, you can't spray for those little guys. They're like the looters, you know, you just gotta keep 'em back at the perimeter.

[KARL *keeps working.* STEVE *gives* SARA *a look, then continues.*]

STEVE: What's your name, sir?

KARL: Huh?

STEVE: What's your name?

KARL: Karl.

STEVE: I'm Steve.

KARL: Nice to meetcha.

STEVE: This is my wife, Sara.

KARL: Hey there.

STEVE: So you're still, uh, working at your age, huh? That's pretty remarkable.

KARL: Yah. I tried to retire, you know, back in the nineties, but I almost went crazy, sitting around the house. Game shows. Gimme a break.

STEVE: I'm just the same way.

SARA: Where are you from, originally?

KARL: Germany.

SARA: Neat. We just moved down here from Minnesota six weeks ago.

STEVE: Mosquito country.

KARL: Yah. I had a cousin up in New Munich once.

SARA: Oh, what's his name?

KARL: He's dead.

SARA: I'm sorry.

KARL: S'okay, it's not your fault.

STEVE: D'ja go to church, growing up, Karl?

KARL: Huh?

STEVE: I said, did you go to church when you were growing up?

KARL: Why?

STEVE: I don't know. Just curious. I've always been interested in people's beliefs.

[*Beat.*]

KARL: Are you a Jesus Freak?

STEVE [*taken aback but amused*]: Uhhh, we're not "Jesus Freaks" . . .

SARA: But we are both committed Christians.

KARL: Well then, I got some news for you.

STEVE: Alright.

KARL: One, there's no Jesus.

STEVE: OK.

KARL: Two, there's no God.

STEVE: Interesting.

KARL: Three, mind your own business and everything works out.

[STEVE *gives* SARA *a look of cheerful complicity: business as usual.*]

STEVE: Can I ask you a question, though, sir?

KARL: No.

STEVE: Do you think the earth just made itself?

KARL: We're gonna talk about the earth now?

SARA [*after a look from* STEVE]: Well, if you really think there's no Creator, then you must think the earth just made itself.

KARL: I don't know who made the earth, Mrs. Jesus Freak, I woke up alive one morning and it's here. I make the best of it.

STEVE: So you must think something can just come out of nothing.

KARL: What?

SARA: If you think there's no Creator, then you must think something can come out of nothing, just like that.

KARL: You know what I think? I think you're both Jesus Freaks and you won't even admit it.

STEVE: Sir, I'll admit a couple things: ONE, I've never seen something come out of nothing AND I've never seen any single thing IN the world that could have MADE the world, so I have to believe the world was created.

KARL: *That's* a bunch of donkey doody.

STEVE: Two.

KARL: That's three.

STEVE: I'll ALSO admit there are historical records proving the existence of a man named Yeshua Ben Joseph or Jesus who was alive at roughly the time the Bible says he was AND I'll admit that, for reasons I can't explain, the stories of his life and death and resurrection effected the most powerful change in the history of mankind that has ever been witnessed and three—

KARL: That's five—

STEVE: Just let me finish—

KARL: Maybe six.

STEVE: I'll admit I was once just like you, with all the same questions and all the same doubts, but one night I humbled myself and asked God to show me whether He existed or not, and He did, He showed me, and my life has not been the same ever since, and if

He can do that for me, He can do it for you, if you want Him to, if your heart's open to it.

KARL: There is no God.

STEVE: How can you be so sure?

KARL: Because I am! I know! It's what it is, I know it!

STEVE: For absolute sure?

KARL: Yah, for absolute sure!

STEVE: See, I don't see how a person can be that sure about anything. I don't.

KARL: I'll tell you, Jesus Freak. When I was a little boy, we lived in Hamburg.

STEVE [*a great fun surprise*]: Oh, you're Jewish, that's great!

KARL: No, I'm not Jewish, Jesus Freak, listen to me! Listen when people talk!

[STEVE *is a bit put off, but* SARA *feels for the guy. A beat.*]

SARA: We're listening.

KARL: When I was little, we lived in Hamburg, and in 1936, before anything that bad had really happened yet with the Nazis, my father sat me down with my brother and he explained to us the Jews. He said, "Children, the Jews are God's secret." He said, "They are a secret God is keeping until the end of time, and we can't know the secret; not even the Jews themselves know the secret, they just ARE the secret. For how can a secret know itself?"

STEVE [*half to* SARA]: That's a good point.

KARL: So my father said, "Children, no matter what Hitler does, no matter what that fucker Hitler does, we are going to help the Jews.

We are going to keep God's secret because it is mysterious and right." So, during the course of the war, we hid Jews in our attic, we hid Jews in our basement, they were everywhere!

[*A beat.*]

My first kiss was from a Jewish girl named Rachel who came to stay with us after her parents were taken to the camps, and we kissed one night, because she was scared and sleeping on the floor and she asked to get in bed with me. Twelve years old, and she kissed me on the cheek.

[*A moment passes.* KARL *grows angry and sad, remembering.*]

How many Jews did we save? How many secrets did we keep for your "God"? And then the Allies start bombing. They knew where the camps were, they knew where the soldiers were, but they bombed Hamburg. This was the great American plan. I saw my mother on fire, Jesus Freak. I saw my father cut into half, two pieces, when a piano fell on him, from the floor above. I am the only one in the family who survived. And my little friend Rachel . . .

[*A beat.*]

After the bombing, the Nazis come. They find me hiding in the basement. They say, "Is there anyone else here?" And I say, "No." But then, they push the bayonet point in my eye—I still don't see so well from this eye—and they say, "Is anyone else here?" And I say, "Yah," and I point to the, uh, you know, the cistern. Well, they pull her out of there, Rachel, and they rape her in front of me. Then they make me rape her in front of them. And then they take her away to the camps.

SARA: I'm sorry.

KARL: Ever since then, I know two things for sure. I know there's no God. There's no one watching the world, or keeping anything from happening. And, worse, I know my father is a fool. He is someone who makes himself foolish living for a lie.

[*The process of reloading from the camera is complete.* SAM *fills with emotion, seeing something on the screen and waving to it.*]

SAM: Hello.

[SAM *starts to cry a little.* STEVE's *cell phone rings.*]

STEVE [*gently but clearly*]: You don't see God's grace at work in that story, sir?

SARA: Steve . . .

STEVE: You really don't?

KARL: No, I don't.

[*The phone rings again.* STEVE *takes it from his pocket.*]

STEVE: Who gave your father the compassion to reach out to those people, sir? Who saved your life?

KARL: Who killed everyone I know?

[*The phone rings again.* STEVE *looks at the caller ID.*]

STEVE [*to* KARL]: Hold that thought.

[STEVE *puts the phone to his ear and speaks into it.*]

Hello.

SCENE 3

[*The time is a few days later.* SAM, *still bandaged but without the arm sling, is sitting at the dining room table with his laptop open and the camera nearby. He is talking on the phone, frustrated.*]

SAM: YES. I was saving the images on the memory cards as backups, but also in iPhoto on my hard drive. But every time I shut down the computer and restarted it, I'd go back to iPhoto and the pictures would be gone. Yes. Gone. The window opens and there is nothing there. Thank you.

[SAM *waits, clicking on images with his mouse.*]

Fuck.

[*A beat.*]

[*Into the phone*] Yes, hi. My name is Sam Gavin, my case code is 4-3-7-4-5-1-5-1, and I've got a problem. Well, Angela, I can explain. I have a Nikon D800—thank you, it is a nice camera—and what happened was, I took a great number of pictures with it and I imported them—about seven hundred—and I imported them from the memory cards into your program. A MacBook Pro. Thank you, I appreciate your solidarity, you rock on too. Yeah, I called Apple and they told me that this was a problem with iPhoto and to contact you directly. Yeah, so here's the deal. Every time I import the pictures and then, at some point, shut down the computer and restart it, I open iPhoto and the pictures are gone. No, I open iPhoto, I go to the event, and there's nothing there. Yes, even if I put them on the desktop or try to hide them in some other directory, I come back the next time and they're gone. I know. Yeah, I know. It is strange. OK, thank you.

[*There are two knocks.*]

SARA [*offstage*]: Mr. Gavin?

[*Again,* SAM *does not respond.*]

SAM: But if I have to tell another person this story *after* I talk to your manager, I'm going to kill somebody. Thank you. I appreciate that. "Angela."

[SAM *waits. A moment later,* SARA *enters her own condo carrying a bag of pastries and two coffees from Starbucks in a carrier. She sets them down and sits, staring at the coffees dejectedly.*]

SAM [*into the phone*]: Yes, hi. 4-3-7-4-5-1-5-1. Well, Dave, let me ask you a question before we get into this, because perhaps you can just help me. Is it possible for memory cards to have pictures on them but look like they're empty when you try to open them up? A Nikon D800.

[SARA, *steeling herself, stands up, takes the coffees and pastries, and exits out the door, closing it behind her.*]

SAM [*into the phone*]: That is a long story, actually, that I am not especially interested in telling again, the point, Dave, is my pictures in
iPhoto keep disappearing, and honestly, that wouldn't really even
be such a problem if I knew I still had them on the memory cards.
I'd be happy to let your idiotic program pretend to upload my pictures every day as long as I knew they were still on the memory
cards where I could retrieve them, but now, all of a sudden, when
I go back to the memory cards to upload them again after they've
been mysteriously vanquished by your program, the memory
cards are empty, even though I didn't elect to delete the files when
I uploaded the images in the first place. No, I didn't elect to delete
to them, are you listening to me, I saved them on the cards, but
when I go back to get them, the pictures aren't there unless you
tell me they could possibly be hiding on the memory cards some-
where but the directory for some reason doesn't see them because
someone didn't know what the fuck they were doing when they
wrote the format code for the disk?

[*There is a knock at the door.*]

I already talked to SanDisk and they said the problem is you! I'm
sorry I'm speaking in this tone of voice, but I took a trip to Italy
with my fiancée, Dave, and we took seven hundred pictures of the
best moments of my motherfucking life that I'll never ever ever
have back again—

[*There are more knocks at the door.*]

SARA: Mr. Gavin?

SAM:—because now she's dead and all I have left are these pictures
that your stupid fucking community college programmers have
kidnapped, hold on a second!

[SAM *rises and rushes to the door, opens it.* SARA *is standing there with her coffees and pastries in a bag.*]

SAM: Mrs. Hutchinson!

SARA: Yeah, hi.

SAM: I'm not going to waste your time with a lot of politeness right now.

SARA: Uhh, OK.

SAM: I want you to leave me alone. Stop knocking on my door. Stop leaving little notes on my doorstep. Stop trying to be friends.

SARA: OK.

SAM: I don't want your charity, I don't want your pity, and I certainly don't want any more of your dry-ass cookies.

SARA: I wasn't trying to bother you.

SAM: I didn't say you were, don't twist what I said, I'm trying to be nice, good-bye.

[SAM *slams the door in* SARA'*s face and then, after a beat, opens it.* SARA *is still standing there, blown away.*]

And if you'd really like to help, turn down that Christian music you play all the time! What are you, fucking deaf?

[SAM *slams the door in* SARA'*s face and goes back to the table and sits.*]

Hello?

[*There's no one on the other end of the line.*]

Fuck.

[SAM *throws the phone across the room.* SARA *enters, shaken, and sits down beside* SAM *at the table. If they were in the same room, they'd be looking at each other.* SAM *screams.*]

Fuuuccckkk!

[SARA *turns and looks at the wall, hearing it from* SAM's *condo. She takes a coffee and drinks a few sips. Time passes.* SARA *rises and goes to a side table, pulls out a condo directory, and dials.* SAM's *cell phone rings. He rises and goes to it and sees who's calling.*]

SAM: Jesus Christ.

[SAM *answers.*]

Hello?

SARA: Mr. Gavin, this is Sara Hutchinson from next door. I won't bother you anymore after this. I just want you to know, I'm not trying to be charitable or pitying or anything. My husband works all day and I'm all alone here and I don't know anyone because we've just moved down here from Minnesota and since you're around a lot too, I thought we could be friends. It's not charity. I really don't appreciate being talked to like that.

SAM: Uhh . . .

SARA: And I will try to be more aware of the volume I play my music at.

SAM: Hi.

SARA: Hi.

SAM: Hi.

[*A moment passes.*]

That was a bad conversation.

SARA: Yes it was.

SAM: You, uh, you just caught me at a bad time.

SARA: I'm sorry.

SAM: I'm sorry, too. I'm having some computer troubles and I was in Tech Support Hell when you knocked, and they weren't being of much assistance, which they rarely are, and . . . anyway, I'm sorry.

[*A moment passes.*]

SARA: Mac or PC?

SAM: Mac.

SARA: Oh.

SAM: You're PC?

SARA: Yeah.

SAM: I figured.

[*A moment passes while* SARA *and* SAM *deal with the impasse.*]

SARA: Have you tried just turning it off and turning it on again?

SCENE 4

[*It's a few weeks later.* STEVE, SARA, *and* SAM *(still bandaged) are drinking iced tea in tall glasses.*]

STEVE: Mr. Himmelman and his partners in Zurich have a fund of fourteen million dollars they've allocated for the purchase of this hotel, and *their* rate of return in year two is currently looking to be just under three million.

SAM: Jesus.

STEVE [*uncomfortable with the word*]: Yeah.

SAM: That sounds kinda unrealistic.

STEVE: I know! But that's the math! These tertiary markets are just blowin' up, Sam! People fly in to do business in the urban centers and their companies don't want to pay for the downtown hotels so they put 'em up in the suburbs—it's a sign of a struggling economy but it's good business for us.

SAM: And so you guys—

[STEVE *scratches his body periodically throughout the scene.* SAM *notices.*]

Are you alright?

STEVE [*minimizing*]: Yeah, I'm fine, Sam, thanks, what's the question?

SAM: So you guys—this is the business you were in when you lived in St. Paul?

STEVE: Sorta. We had a hotel renovation company up there, had a little office, and worked doing renovations all over the country for owners who, say, wanted to buy an old Residence Inn and turn it into a Candlewood Suites or something like that. We'd work with the new franchise to make sure the renovation would conform to their specs, we'd send our wallpaper and carpet crews out to do the work, that was it.

SAM: But then you—

STEVE: But then things got interesting.

[STEVE *looks to* SARA *and gives her an excited look, then continues.*]

I met this money manager at Promise Keepers named Gary Oliver who heard about the business I was in, and he told me he had an investor in Zurich named Mr. Himmelman who was looking for an investment opportunity in the hospitality industry in order to diversify his portfolio. Well, I shared with Gary a vision I'd been given by the Lord a few years back to start a chain of gospel-themed hotels—

SAM: Gospel-themed hotels . . . ?

STEVE: Yeah. Gospel-themed hotels, Sam. Every one with a sanctuary. Baptismal pool. Jungle gym, for the little monkeys. High-speed Internet. Video-conferencing. Promise Keepers strength training. Full-on gospel hotels. "Where Would Jesus Stay?"

SAM: That wouldn't be my type of thing.

STEVE: I've heard, but Mr. Himmelman liked it. So he gave me ten thousand dollars to pay for the due diligence of locating a property in a tertiary market with an eye to buying the property and building the template, so Sara and I found this old Sheraton, it was tied up in receivership, so we initiated a conversation with the bank, signed the purchase agreement, and here we are.

SAM: What's it gonna be called?

STEVE: "Crossroads Inns."

SARA: Steve.

STEVE: She doesn't like the name, but here's the point, Sam.

SAM: OK.

STEVE: This idea, whether *you* like it or not yet, is gonna make a lotta money. God wants it to happen. So. Keep that in the back of your mind.

SAM: OK. [*A joke, for* SARA*'s benefit*] It's back there.

[STEVE *clocks that intimacy but figures it's in his best interest.*]

STEVE: Anyway, the *other* win side of this win–win equation is ours, or, potentially, yours—

SAM: OK—

STEVE:—because my company is gonna get paid by the LLC to do the renovation, and then, as part owners, we're gonna get a cut of the sale when it's sold.

SAM: To who?

STEVE: What do you mean?

SAM: Who are you planning on selling this gospel hotel to once you've built it?

STEVE: I don't know, somebody. That's the Lord's problem, Sam, it's not mine. I just know I'm not in the hotel business, I'm in the hotel renovation business, so I'm gonna take the money and run and collect the franchise fees on the back end for the next thirty years or however much the Lord lets me have.

SAM: Gotcha.

STEVE: So your rate of return in year two wouldn't be twenty percent like Mr. Himmelman's, but it would be seventeen, which is still a lot better than you're gonna do on the market.

SAM: And this is legal?

STEVE: Totally.

SAM: Jesus. [*To* SARA] You can really pay yourself to pay yourself like that?

SARA: Apparently so.

SAM [*still reasoning it out*]: Alright . . .

STEVE: You want in?

SAM: No, I'm still just trying to understand something . . .

STEVE: Shoot. I love to answer questions about this project.

SAM: . . . you DO need money right now . . . or you DON'T?

STEVE: I DON'T.

[*A long beat.*]

But I DO, in the sense that I AM in a little bit of a cash-flow crunch, just this week all of a sudden.

SAM: Because . . .

STEVE: Because . . . well, for instance, I'll give you an example. I've got these wallpaper and carpet crews from Minnesota down here ready to start work, right? Chomping at the bit. Got 'em down here the day after Mr. Himmelman signed off on the purchase. And the good news is the fact they're down here already is gonna represent a tremendous savings when we do get started, because of transportation costs and readiness, but for now they need to be paid.

SAM: They're not being paid?

STEVE: Well, no, I was paying them, for the first few weeks, but then it kinda became untenable, so I told 'em it was up to them whether they wanted to stick around or not, and I've been working with these guys for years, you know, they believe in me, so they're still living down here.

SARA: Sort of living.

SAM: What does that mean?

STEVE: Oh, all she means, Sam, is, and I'm embarrassed to say this, but some of these guys are now basically living in their cars.

SAM: Living in their cars?

SARA: Mmhmm.

STEVE: Basically.

SAM: Jesus.

STEVE: I mean, not even basically, let's just say it, they're living in their cars.

SAM: Where?

STEVE: Just down the street. Many can't read. And they need to be paid a little something in the interim, right, while we wait for the money to come through? It's only fair. So, ultimately, do *I* need the money? No. Is this a great moment for a partner to get in on the ground floor and reap some really impressive returns? And help out some really sweet guys who are kind of in a bind in the bargain? *You* have to decide.

[*A beat.*]

You can meet the guys if you want.

SARA: They're very sweet.

SAM: No, that's OK. I get it.

STEVE: So you want in?

SAM: No, I was just saying I think I finally get it now.

STEVE [*masking disappointment*]: Yeah. It is kinda complicated when you don't know the hotel renovation business. It's a very specific . . . creature.

[*A moment passes while* STEVE *scratches and* SAM *watches.*]

SAM: Steve.

STEVE: Right here. Yeah.

SAM: Explain one last thing to me . . .

STEVE: Shoot.

SAM: And then I'm done quizzing you.

STEVE: Shoot.

SAM: It *sounds* good.

STEVE: It does. Shoot.

SAM: Mr. . . .

STEVE: Himmelman.

SAM: Yeah.

STEVE: Great guy.

SAM: He promised you the money *when* . . . ?

[*A moment passes while* STEVE *seems like he's lost in thought.*]

STEVE: When did he "promise me the money . . ."?

SAM: Yeah, when did he say he was gonna give you this money to buy the hotel in the first place?

[*As* STEVE *explains this, he half looks to* SARA *for confirmation.*]

STEVE: Well, when we still had the renovation company back in Minnesota, he gave me the initial ten thousand dollars . . .

SAM: To locate a suitable property.

STEVE: Right. And then we found it, he approved the purchase; at his command, I signed the purchase agreement with the seller, which in this case was the bank, and he promised he'd wire the money from Zurich in the morning.

SAM: Fourteen million dollars.

STEVE: Right.

SAM: And when did he make that promise?

STEVE: Twenty-nine days ago.

SAM: Twenty-nine days ago?

STEVE: Yeah, but it's coming.

SAM: So you signed the purchase agreement when you didn't have any money whatsoever?

STEVE: Totally.

SAM: Why?

STEVE: Why what?

SAM: Why did you go ahead and sign the purchase agreement when you didn't yet have the actual money to purchase the property?

STEVE: Because Mr. Himmelman told me to. It's his money, not mine.

SAM: But it's your name on the purchase agreement.

STEVE: Yeah, it's gotta be, I'm the majority partner in the LLC.

SAM: And the bank let you sign the purchase agreement without wiring them any money on the day of purchase?

STEVE: Yeah.

SAM: Why?

STEVE: Because they wanna get rid of it and no one else wants to buy it. And there was a holiday in Switzerland. It was, like, a grace period. No one cared.

SAM: But no money has *ever* been wired. *Ever.*

STEVE: No.

SAM: Jesus.

STEVE: But it will be.

SAM: How do you *know*?

STEVE [*like an ace in the hole*]: Because Mr. Himmelman's on the hook for it. He promised me. I promised them. It's all legally binding. It'd be kinda stupid not to follow through. Don't worry about me, Sam. He'll send it.

SAM: You trust him?

STEVE: Totally.

[SAM *and* SARA *exchange a brief look of shared incredulity.*]

SAM: But Steve . . .

STEVE: Yeah.

SAM: If this Mr. Himmelman's the one who got you into this predicament . . .

STEVE: Yeah?

SAM: Why can't you just ask HIM to advance you some money against the eventual income you're all gonna make off the sale of this property?

STEVE: Because I don't want to.

[*A beat.*]

See, Sam, you're a scientist. You're, like, an athlete of the mind, and that's great. You, with your great mind, you can compute things I can't even imagine, probably that *most* people can't. What a gift. My expertise, Sam, my gift that I've been given . . . is faith. See, I'm not a knower. I'm a believer. And that's what real estate is all about. It's about faith. It's about the substance of things not seen. Is the money here? Is the money there? It doesn't matter. I don't care. What matters is, can you sit down with people and imagine possibilities? Can you sit down with the city fathers and imagine turning a run-down Comfort Inn into a Holiday Inn Express with a pool? Can you imagine turning a pathetic, drug-infested, big-city block into a glittering new mall with a Hilton Hotel as the centerpiece and a Starbucks and a Pinkberry and a Hard Rock Cafe? If you can imagine that kinda stuff in my business, Sam, you're not just halfway there, you're all the way, because the money doesn't matter. It does not matter. The work of real-estate development and especially hotel development—it's so important—is belief. That's what I'm talking about. Belief. Don't invest in this hotel. Don't. Please. Don't. Invest in believing. Invest in the believing part of yourself.

[*A long moment passes.*]

SAM: How much do you need?

STEVE: Right now?

SAM: Yeah.

STEVE: Seventy-five.

SAM: Thousand . . . ?

STEVE: Or ten.

SAM: Seventy-five thousand or ten?

STEVE: Well, like I said, Sam, it's just a cash-flow problem right now. If I can get a Band-Aid, I'll take a Band-Aid. If I can get a partner, I'll take a partner.

[*A moment passes.*]

SARA: You don't have to answer right now.

SAM: *Can* I think about it a little bit . . . ?

STEVE: Think about it all you want. I think it's a good opportunity. If you don't, you don't. If you do, you do. Time is of the essence. But sure. Think about it. I mean, we didn't ask you over here to sell you something.

[*A moment passes.* STEVE *scratches.*]

SAM: Are you sure you're alright there . . . ?

STEVE: Yeah, I've just got a little . . . rash lately. Kinda maybe shingles. I don't know. It'll pass.

SAM: Maybe you should go see a doctor . . . ?

[*A moment passes while* STEVE *scratches.*]

SARA: Sam's work at NASA's pretty interesting.

STEVE: Yeah, what exactly is it they've got you doing over there? Sara's tried to explain it to me, but it just sounds so complicated . . .

SAM: Well, what I've been doing for the past ten years *is* kinda complicated to explain. I tend to talk about it with people in terms of plumbing.

STEVE [*making a joke*]: So you're a space plumber.

SAM: Kinda. See, we all have these probes, you know, out in the solar system.

STEVE: We do? I do?

SAM: No, I mean, we at NASA have all these probes . . .

STEVE: Oh, yeah, yeah, I've read about this.

SAM: Well, they're collecting information all the time with sensors of various kinds, some of this information coming from, essentially, the beginning of time, and they send that information back to Earth through space on these data streams which we catch, kinda like water coming into the house through a pipe, into the sink of the system, which is the NASA network.

STEVE [*to* SARA]: See, he's a thinker. [*To* SAM] It's great.

SAM: Anyway, to make a long story short, the data streams, as they go through space, get interfered with by radio waves, X-rays, all kinds of energy, so it's like there's always garbage in the pipes, slowing down the data . . .

STEVE: So it is a lot like plumbing.

SAM: Yeah—

STEVE: That's great—

SAM: So my job is to try to find new ways to seal those data streams and keep the interference out, so we can get as much pure information from the beginning of time coming into the system as quickly as possible.

STEVE: I loved *Apollo 13*.

SAM: It's not very accurate.

STEVE: I don't care—

SAM: No, nobody does.

STEVE [*overlapping with above*]:—I'll see anything Tom Hanks is in.

SARA: He's our favorite.

SAM: But that's the thing, Steve, that's what space is to most people, it's *Apollo 13*. "Tom Hanks." *2001*. It's "*outer* space." To me, in my job, space is *space*. It's distance.

STEVE: Ohhhh. Yeah. I getcha now.

SAM: Space is a tremendous distance that you have to get information across *in time.* That's the problem with space.

STEVE: Time.

SAM: Yes. How can we know what we need to know—in time—when what we need to know has to come from *so* far away?

STEVE: How can you?

SAM: You can't. Ultimately. You can know some, but not all of it. Not in time.

[*A moment passes.*]

There's always gonna be some information that comes in a little too late.

STEVE [*making a mental note*]: Huh.

[*A beat.*]

That's fascinating.

[*A moment passes.* SAM *and* SARA *exchange a look.* SAM *makes up his mind about something.*]

SAM: Hang on a second.

[SAM *rises and heads for the door.*]

SARA: Sam . . . ?

STEVE: Everything alright?

SAM: Yeah, I'm just . . . Hang on.

[SAM *exits and the door closes behind him.*]

SARA: Why did you do that?

STEVE: Why did I do what . . . ?

SARA: Ask him for money.

STEVE: You told me to tell him about the project.

SARA: Yeah, but not to ask him for money the first day you meet him—

STEVE: Sorry! It seemed like that's where the Spirit was leading, I—

[*A beat.*]

—you think he's upset?

[*A key turns and* SAM *enters, unseen by* STEVE *and* SARA, *and goes into his kitchen and then his bedroom.*]

SARA: I don't know. He gets moody sometimes. He gets kinda—overcome. He only lost his fiancée, like, five or six months ago.

STEVE: He's the one that started talking about *time* and *space*—

SARA: I know that!

STEVE: I didn't bring *that* stuff up!

SARA: I don't think that was the problem, I just think—

STEVE: I mean, I like the guy, Sara, I don't care if he invests or not—

SARA: You do?

STEVE: Yeah, I mean, sure, it'd be ideal if he could, you know, but ultimately, I mean, maybe you should go over and make sure he knows that, you know, that it's all OK either way. The last thing I wanna do is pressure the guy. It's not right and it's not good business. Maybe you should go—

[SAM *comes out of the bedroom and goes to the door.*]

SARA: No, just give him a chance.

STEVE: What do you think he's doing over there?

SARA: I don't know.

STEVE: You think he's crying?

SARA: I don't know.

STEVE: I feel like I've heard him crying sometimes.

SARA: I don't know.

STEVE: Poor guy.

[SAM *exits, shutting the door behind him.*]

Does he have to use his own bathroom because of the accident?

SARA: I don't think so.

STEVE: Maybe he needs to sit on something soft, or, I don't know, when he goes?

[*There's a knock at the door.*]

You get it.

SARA: You can get it.

STEVE: You're his friend, Sara, get it. [*Becoming more insistent as* SARA *hesitates*] Get it!

[SARA *rises, goes to the door, and opens it.* SAM *is there.*]

SAM: Hey.

SARA: Hi.

[SAM *heads back toward his seat.*]

We were a little worried—

SAM: No, no need—

STEVE: Sara was afraid I maybe came on a little too strong there—

SAM: No, not at all, Steve, not at all.

[STEVE *gives* SARA *a look.*]

    It's all good.

[SAM *sits down.* SARA *sits down.* SAM *looks at* STEVE.]

    I can do fifty.

STEVE: Thousand?

SAM: Yeah.

SARA: You don't have to.

STEVE: He knows—

SAM: Yeah, I know I don't have to. I want to. I want to help.

[*A beat.*]

STEVE: I don't know what to say. Praise God.

[SAM *takes out his checkbook.*]

SAM: From my point of view, Steve, you're the one doing me a favor.

STEVE: I know, but come on, fifty thousand dollars, Sam, that's, uh, that's a big—

SAM: It's, it's fine, I'm just happy to do something helpful with some of this insurance money. Get it off my . . . conscience a little.

[SARA *notes this phrase.* SAM *opens his checkbook.*]

So to whom do I make this out?

STEVE: Sonrise Hotels, LLC.

SARA: With an O.

[*A beat.*]

SAM: Oh. OK.

[*As* SAM *writes the check,* STEVE *gets an idea.*]

STEVE: Can I ask you a question, Sam?

SAM: Sure. One sec.

[SAM *tears out the check, hands it to* STEVE.]

STEVE: Dja go to church, growing up?

SAM [*after a look to* SARA]: Why?

SARA: Steve.

STEVE: I don't know, I'm just always curious about people's beliefs. It's interesting to me.

SARA: Steve, maybe you shouldn't—

STEVE: If he doesn't want to talk about it, that's fine. It's just a question, Sara. [*To* SAM] Right? It's just a conversation. Dja go to church, growing up?

[*A beat.*]

SAM: Unitarian-Universalist.

STEVE: Oh. Nice. Nice.

SAM: We didn't go much, though.

STEVE: Yeah, probably not.

[*A beat.*]

They're the ones that think Jesus is, just, like, a "good guy," right? Not the Son of God or anything like that.

SAM: I think they leave it kinda open to whatever people think.

STEVE: Yeah, they do. That's kinda their thing.

SAM: Yep.

STEVE: And so, do you think that's what Jesus was . . . a good guy?

SAM: Honestly?

STEVE: Please.

SAM: I don't think much about Jesus one way or the other.

STEVE: Oh, really? Because you say His name a lot.

SAM [*amused*]: It's just a figure of speech.

STEVE: OH. Well, you should know, just as an informed person, that that's not who Jesus said He was. Jesus didn't say He was a good guy, or a figure of speech. He said He was the Son of God. The Way, the Truth, and the Life. "The reflection of God's glory and the exact imprint of God's very being who sustains all things by his powerful word," Hebrews, chapter one, verse three.

SAM: OK.

STEVE: But that's not who you think He is, is it? Even though that's what He said.

[*A moment passes.*]

SAM: Do you really want to have this conversation right now?

STEVE: Yeah, why not? It's just a conversation. I'm not trying to change anybody. I just think it's interesting. You're obviously a very intelligent person, Sam, much smarter than me. I just want to know what you think.

[SAM *and* SARA *exchange a look. A beat.*]

SAM: Alright. Uhh, I think Jesus . . .

STEVE: Yeah? Just be honest.

SAM: I think Jesus was probably someone who actually lived and died and did some impressive things, politically and personally. And today I think he is a mythical figure used by charlatans and multinational corporate churches to extort money from people who find life too difficult to face without hearing some lie every Sunday morning, like, "It's all gonna work out," or "God's on your side," or something like that.

STEVE: So you're mad at God.

SAM: No, I'm mad at people who suck money and life out of other people in the name of some idea about God that isn't true—

STEVE: But you think there's a God.

SAM: I don't know if there's a God. My guess is there probably isn't.

STEVE: But if there is one, He must be letting all this happen, right? I mean, if there is a God, then He must be letting these people suck the money and life out of other people in the name of an idea about God that isn't true.

[*A beat.*]

SAM: I guess so.

STEVE: And that makes you mad.

SAM: Yeah.

STEVE: So just admit it, you're mad at God for religious hypocrisy.

SAM: But I don't think there's a God to be mad at.

STEVE: And you're mad about that too. You're mad there's no one up there to *stop* these people from spreading these lies.

SAM: I guess so.

STEVE: Which is the same as being mad at God!

SAM: No, it's not the same at all!

STEVE [*overlapping*]: Sure it is, Sam—

SARA: Steve—

STEVE: Sara, wouldja please?

SARA: Sorry.

STEVE [*to* SAM]: You're mad at God for not existing! Just say it! You're mad at God for not existing! You're mad at God for religious hypocrisy! You're mad at God for letting kids in Africa starve to death and get AIDS, probably, any smart person would be. You're probably mad at God that people have to die at all. You're mad at God for killing your fiancée. And you're mad at God for what He's done to your face. Just admit it, Sam. It's OK. You're allowed to say it. Just say it. You're mad at God.

SAM: You'd be mad too, if you woke up tomorrow without her in your life, and, uh, with a face that looks like this.

STEVE: Sam, my mother dropped dead in front of me when I was seven. I had three awful stepmothers, one of whom got drunk one night and tried to kill me. I had to leave home at fourteen, I lived on the road for, like, five years, with everybody I ran into wanting something from me—

SAM: Sorry.

STEVE: That's not the point! The point is, I had a lot to be mad about too. I HAVE a lot to be mad about. We all do. Being human sucks!

[STEVE *finally reins it in a bit.*]

But then one night I went out under the stars, all alone—

SAM: And found your precious loving Jesus, I know.

STEVE: It's not as stupid as you make it wanna sound! In fact, you and I both know the only reason you make it sound so stupid is, Sam, if it sounded any smarter, you'd have to believe it too!

SAM: You know what . . . give me my check back. [*To* SARA] I'm sorry.

STEVE: You're lying to yourself, Sam.

SAM: Give me back my check.

STEVE: You talk about all these distances you can never get across in time, "Oh, poor us, space and time, it's so *far.*" When you're in the Lord, Sam, there is no space and time. Everyone knows everything, it's all just *there.*

SAM: Give me my fucking check!

STEVE: Don't pretend you don't know moments like that happen!

SAM: Give me my check!!

STEVE: Here! Take it! Fine!

[STEVE *gives the check back to* SAM.]

Your eternal salvation's a heck of a lot more important to me than some hotel! It is! But see, that's why you *oughta* invest in it. And that's why you oughta trust me when I say you need to get to know the Lord.

SAM: GET! OUT!

SARA: Sam.

SAM: What?

SARA: This is *our* place.

SCENE 5

[*It's one month later.* SAM *and* SARA *are sitting on the sofa. There are three photos and a large Tupperware container of soup on the coffee table.* SARA *is reciting a poem from memory.*]

SARA: "J'errais donc, l'oeil rivé sur le pavé vieilli
Quand avec du soleil aux cheveux, dans la rue
Et dans le soir, tu m'es en riant apparue
Et j'ai cru voir la fée au chapeau de clarté
Qui jadis sur mes beaux sommeils d'enfant gâté
Passait, laissant toujours de ses mains mal fermées
Neiger de blancs bouquets d'étoiles parfumées."

SAM: What does it mean?

[SARA *translates it as haltingly as she said it in French.*]

SARA: "I wandered then, my eyes on the worn pavement, when you, in the street, in the evening appeared to me, and I thought I saw the fairy with her cap of brightness, who once on the beauty sleeps of my spoiled childhood passed, letting always her half-closed hands snow down white bouquets of perfumed stars."

[*A moment passes.* SARA *feels shy.*]

SAM: You should really get back and do that.

SARA: Maybe. Someday.

[*A beat.*]

    I kinda got off course.

[SARA *looks at one of the pictures.*]

    Where *is* Wesleyan, anyway?

SAM: Macon, Georgia. There's a Wesleyan in Connecticut, too, but that's the university. She went to the college.

[SARA *looks at the pictures and doesn't know what to say next. Beat.*]

SARA: There are all these schools I hear about all the time, but I have no idea where they are. Like . . . Brown, where is Brown?

SAM: Providence.

SARA: Or Temple?

SAM: Philadelphia.

SARA: So you know where every little private school is?

SAM: No, I think it's regional. Most of the small private schools are in the east. You're not from the east.

[*A beat.*]

    The math is against you.

SARA: Where's Smith?

SAM: Northampton.

SARA: Where's Vassar?

SAM: Poughkeepsie.

SARA: Where's Loomer?

SAM: I don't know.

SARA: I just made that up. [*After a twinkle*] Where did you go to school?

SAM: MIT.

SARA: I know where that is.

[*A long look happens which* SAM *eventually breaks.*]

SAM [*referring to the photo*]: Those two girls there, those were her best friends from college. That's Kara and that's Cammy.

SARA: How did you guys meet?

SAM: The Internet.

SARA: Really?

SAM: Yeah. She was a friend of a friend on Facebook and I poked her. How did you two meet?

SARA: At church. There used to be this church in downtown Minneapolis that had their worship services in, like, this huge old sorta Broadway-type theater, and we met there during a Bible Study group for singles.

SAM: How long ago?

SARA: About six years, I guess. Seven. And we were the only people in the group who smoked, and so we sorta met that way.

SAM: You don't smoke now, though, do you?

SARA: No, neither one of us do, we quit.

[*A beat.*]

   We quit together.

[*A moment while* SAM *looks at a picture.*]

SAM: This one's gotten tremendously fat. Since this picture.

SARA: Because she had a baby?

SAM: Why do you say that?

SARA: I don't know. I always wonder, if I ever have a baby, will I be the type who can never get back to the pre-baby weight.

SAM: I think you'll be fine.

[*A beat.*]

   They really didn't like that I took her away from Atlanta. They always gave me a hard time about that. But I couldn't live in the same town as her mother. It was too much.

SARA [*referring to a picture*]: She skated.

SAM: Yeah. She skated. She played flute. She was a great person. Very light.

SARA: She seems like it.

[*A moment passes.*]

   I wish I could have known her. We could have all been neighbors.

[*A moment passes.*]

Did you two want to have kids?

[*A beat.*]

Is that OK to ask?

SAM: Yeah, it's fine. We wanted to, but she couldn't.

SARA: Oh.

SAM: She was diabetic and it had kinda screwed up her system.

SARA: Do you still want to have kids? Someday?

SAM: Sure. I mean, it doesn't seem too likely at this point, but . . . sure.

[*A moment passes.*]

So . . . that's it.

[*He gathers up the photos.*]

That's all I got left. Thanks to digital.

SARA: Thank you for showing me.

SAM: Of course.

[*A moment passes.*]

I'm thinking maybe you shouldn't come over here anymore.

[SARA'*s caught completely off guard.*]

SARA: OK. Can I ask why?

SAM [*overlapping*]: Sure, I—

SARA [*overlapping*]: I mean, am I allowed to ask why, or is this a proc-lamation from on high, that I'm just supposed to obey?

SAM [*overlapping*]: I don't know, am I allowed to finish?

SARA: Yeah, finish, please. Finish.

SAM: I think you coming over here and us spending time together like we've been doing isn't a good idea.

SARA: You really think this . . . ?

SAM: Yeah.

SARA: You said yesterday was the best day you've had since—

SAM [*overlapping*]: It was.

SARA: But today's totally different?

SAM: Yeah.

SARA: Today is *that* different from yesterday.

SAM: Yes, Sara, because of yesterday! *Because* of yesterday! Things happen in order!

[*A beat.*]

I'm trying to stop wasting your time.

SARA: So why didn't you just call and tell me not to come over?

SAM: Because I thought I could enjoy being with you one last time—

SARA: But you can't.

SAM: Not really—

SARA: Not even *knowing* it's the last time—

SAM: No.

[*A moment passes.*]

SARA: Then I feel kinda stupid.

SAM: I'm sorry.

SARA: Sitting here with my stupid soup. And talking French.

[SARA *looks around the room.*]

SAM: I'm sorry.

[*A moment passes.*]

Wouldja just . . . go?

SARA: No.

SAM: Please?

SARA: No. I think you owe me a little more after all this than just "go
home."

SAM [*overlapping*]: I don't owe you anything.

SARA [*overlapping*]: That's so easy to say!

SAM [*overlapping*]: I don't!

SARA [*overlapping*]: Yes, that's the easiest thing in the world to say and
it's almost never true. People do owe each other something—

SAM [*overlapping*]: Sara, you came over here and forced yourself into
my life, I don't owe you!

SARA [*intense*]: OK then, I want more, OK? I don't deserve it, I'm not
owed it, I just want it!

SAM: I want a lot of things too, you can't always get what you want!

[*Beat.*]

SARA [*making a joke*]: Did you really just say that?

SAM: I did!

[*A beat.*]

It's true. You can't.

[*For a moment, it looks like an amiable truce has been reached.*]

SARA: You don't really want me to go.

SAM: Yes I do.

SARA: And not come back . . . not ever?

SAM: I don't think it's good.

SARA: What's not good?

SAM: I need to move on with my life, Sara, you need to move on with yours—

SARA [*giving up, feeling stupid*]: Alright, alright, perfect, perfect, fine.

[SARA *goes to the coffee table and picks up the soup in the Tupperware.*]

Do you want this, you don't, right, of course you don't, because it's from me, your biggest problem.

SAM: It's not that I don't *want* it—

SARA: I get it, you don't have to explain!

SAM: Everything in my refrigerator for the past two months comes from your house, it's like you're my mother!

SARA: Shut up, OK, I get it, OK, I get it, I get it, I GET IT!

[SARA *throws the soup violently across the room at* SAM. *It hits him and bounces without opening.*]

SAM: Jesus!

[SAM *picks up the Tupperware and sets it down right side up.*]

SARA: When we first moved down here, I hated it. I still don't like it. It's too hot, the people aren't friendly, there are bugs everywhere. But from the day you let me in, it's been better. Not simpler, I know that. But better. It has been. The idea that maybe, just maybe, knowing you might be the reason I came here got my mind off my own stupid life for a second.

SAM: And onto mine.

SARA: That's not all bad. I know nowadays people want to con you and call everything where people actually care about each other "codependent" but it's not always true. We're here in this world together. The idea that we're not at all in any way somehow here "for" each other but just somehow "beside" each other is just stupid. If we're here beside each other, we must be here *for* each other a little. A little . . . right?

[*A moment passes.*]

You know, if you asked me to stay and forget this whole conversation right now, I'd be happy to do that. I'd be happy to go back.

[*A moment passes.*]

But I guess we can't. OK. Soup.

[SARA *gets the soup and starts to go.*]

SAM [*overlapping*]: Are you honestly willing to pretend you don't understand?

SARA: I don't know what that means.

SAM: Look at me!

SARA: I'm looking at you!

SAM: No, I mean, really look at me!

SARA: I'm looking! I've been looking!

SAM: You come here every day, as beautiful as anyone I've ever met—

SARA: Don't compliment me while you're throwing me out of your life!

SAM [*overlapping*]: And we have nowhere to go but "friends" or "nurse and fucking patient"! Do you think that's easy for me?

SARA: Do you think it's easy for *me*?

SAM: Sara, look at my face!

SARA: I don't care about your face! How many times would I have to say that to make you understand, Sam? I don't care about your face!

[*A beat.*]

But see, you don't believe that. And *that's* why we can't be together, Sam, it's not your stupid face or me being married or Steve or anything that's happened—anything can happen, things can change—but not if you don't believe that you can be loved *just because you exist.*

[*A long moment passes.*]

SAM: The day she died . . .

SARA: Yeah?

SAM: The day she died, we were supposed to drive up to Atlanta for her mom's birthday. But I wouldn't drive because I thought her mother was such a bitch, I didn't think we should even go. And my opinion was so important. But she wanted to go, and so I said, "Fine, fuck it, we'll go, but I'm not driving." So she drove. Which she hated to do on the highway, because it scared her. But I made her do it. And we had only been on the road for twenty minutes or so when she looked over at me. She was crying. And all I said was, "You wanted to go," and looked away. "You wanted to go."

[*A beat.*]

And then this bright shiny tanker truck pulled up alongside us and I remember, I could hear her crying, but I was pretending I didn't hear, so I was watching the front wheels of the truck go by, as it passed us. And they were strobing, you know? They looked like they were going backwards. And I was thinking, "What's the etymology of that word? *Strobe*. I should really look that up." Because it was easier to think about that than to think about her crying and how I didn't really want to make it better.

[*A moment passes.*]

I just hate it that I'm here and she's not. It's so wrong.

SARA: No it's not.

SAM: Yes it is. It's all wrong. I'm wrong. The fact there's still a me is wrong.

[*A moment passes.*]

SARA: Sam.

SAM: What?

SARA: Can I tell you something?

SAM: I suppose, sure . . .

[*A beat.*]

SARA: When I was thirteen, I went to Bible Camp.

SAM [*getting ready to be skeptical*]: Bible Camp. OK, fuck . . .

SARA: This is not about me wanting to change you or anything, Sam, or convert you, it's just about me, wouldja listen?

SAM: No.

SARA: Sam, I'm not Steve, wouldja just listen?

[*A long beat.*]

SAM: OK.

SARA: When I was thirteen, I went to Bible Camp. And there was a guest speaker at camp all week. His name was Ed Stube. And I went the first night to the big welcome, you know, prayer service, and he was like, "We're all here to have fun and the pancakes'll be good and Jesus, y'know, wow!"

[SAM *laughs a little.*]

And my family, you know, we went to church, but it never really meant anything to me. It was a part of my life, I had friends there, but that was it. But then this guy Ed Stube got up and started showing this slide show about how he was a missionary in Micro-nesia. And he had slides of the countryside and the terraced hills and all that stuff. His church. His congregation. And then up came this slide of, like, a ten-year-old girl.

[*A beat.*]

And I swear, I could feel the elevator drop inside me, just looking in her eyes. Boom. Straight to the bottom. I had no idea why. It just did. But then he said, "This is a girl I raised from the dead."

SAM: And you believed him?

SARA: No, not completely, but the picture was . . . I mean, I had to admit, there was something about it. There was something very weird. There was a fire in the background about ten yards behind her with people all around it. And this girl was in the foreground, staring into the camera. Just a girl. But she had this look in her eyes, Sam. I'd never seen anything like it.

SAM: Do you wanna sit down?

SARA: No. Thank you. Anyway, after the preaching, this guy Ed Stube asked if anyone wanted to come down for the altar call, and, you know, "accept Jesus into their hearts," which is something I never would have done, I didn't even know really what it meant . . . but there was something about that picture. So I did it. I went down and prayed the prayer.

SAM: And you really felt like someone was listening?

SARA: No, not someone. It wasn't a Someone. It was more like Every-thing Else was listening. But it was more than Everything Else, it was like the Everything Else *was* a Someone. Kinda. Somehow. And ever since that night, Sam, I can't help it, there *is* this big music I hear in things, like everything in the world is all one big music and nothing doesn't fit. Nothing doesn't belong. Everything is part of it. Nothing's "wrong."

[*A moment passes.*]

I mean, there's pain. But nothing's *wrong*. Nothing's out of place. Everyone's where they're supposed to be. And it all unfolds.

[SARA *goes over to him, close.*]

And I don't know everything about what you've been, or been like, or what you've done, I just know you now. And I know you don't believe in anything like what I'm talking about, and that's OK. But I want you to know that *I* feel like getting to know you—having the chance—has been a way God has really filled my life with love when I really needed it—and shown me something new and scary and possible, and I'm glad it's happened. I'm glad we've met, I'm glad I came over here.

[*A moment passes.*]

Things can change. They're changing for me. Things can change.

[*A moment passes.*]

SAM: What did you pray? When you prayed? What were the words?

SARA: I don't remember exactly, like, word for word . . .

SAM: But what was the basic idea? I just want to hear what it was.

[*A moment passes.*]

SARA: I'll make you a deal. Do you still have to wear that thing?

SAM: Yeah.

SARA: Really? After all this time? That doesn't make sense.

SAM: I don't want you to see me.

SARA: Come on. It's OK.

SAM: It's not.

SARA: Yeah it is. It's OK. Let me.

[*After a silent visual negotiation,* SARA *reaches up and slowly starts unbandaging* SAM's *face.*]

    Am I hurting?

SAM: No. It's all healed, it's just . . . so fuckin' ugly.

SARA: I bet it's not as bad as you think.

SAM: Why are you doing this?

SARA: Because. I like you.

[SARA *pulls the last of the bandage away.* SAM's *face is, indeed, very badly scarred.* SARA *and* SAM *look at each other for a few moments.*]

    It's not so bad.

[*A moment passes.*]

SAM: So tell me the prayer.

SARA: This won't be exactly it.

SAM: That's alright.

SARA: It'll just be, like you said, sorta the basic idea.

SAM: That's OK.

[*A moment passes.*]

SARA: Dear God.

SAM: Dear God.

SARA: You don't have to say it, I'm just telling you.

SAM: I know.

[*As* SAM *repeats* SARA's *words, it's not as if he's praying. He's experimenting with what it feels like to say it. Conversely,* SARA *is, maybe, customizing the remembered prayer for* SAM. *Maybe not.*]

SARA: Dear God.

SAM: Dear God.

SARA: I don't know why I was born.

SAM: I don't know why I was born.

SARA: I don't know why I have to die.

SAM: I don't know why I have to die.

SARA: I just know there's more of life right now that I need.

SAM: I just know there's more of life right now that I need.

SARA: And I'm asking You to show it to me.

SAM: And I'm asking You to show it to me.

SARA: I know I'm not perfect.

SAM: I know I'm not perfect.

SARA: I don't live up to my own expectations, let alone Yours.

SAM: I don't live up to my own expectations, let alone Yours.

SARA: Please show me Your face.

SAM: Please show me Your face.

SARA: If You're even there.

SAM: If You're even there.

SARA: Please forgive me for the ways I've failed You.

SAM: Please forgive me for the ways I've failed You.

SARA: And I'll forgive You for the ways You've failed me.

SAM [*not part of the prayer*]: Really?

SARA [*likewise*]: Really.

SAM: And I'll forgive You for the ways You've failed me.

SARA: And together we'll start all over.

[STEVE *enters from outside, carrying his briefcase and talking on his cell phone. He scratches when he can. He looks unhealthy.*]

SAM: And together we'll start all over.

STEVE: Look, I've been back and forth with you people about this . . .

SARA: I pray this prayer in the name of Jesus . . .

SAM: I pray this prayer in the name of Jesus . . .

SARA: Your sign to us, in story, of your endless and ever-present love.

SAM: Your sign to us, in story, of your endless and ever-present love.

SARA: Amen.

SAM: Amen.

[SARA *and* SAM *both become aware of a feeling—in them, around them.*]

   [*Half-scared*] Do you feel that?

[*A moment passes.*]

SARA: Yeah.

[SAM *kisses* SARA.]

STEVE: Listen, M-C-S is a recognized condition. Multiple Chemical Sensitivity. [*Into apartment*] Honey? Honey? [*Into phone*] I don't *know* what caused it. My doctor down here sent the materials to the claims person, like, a week ago. Can't you just cover me?

[*A beat.*]

   OK.

[STEVE *sets down the briefcase so he can scratch.*]

   So let's just say I'm having those problems now, and we'll pretend I never *called* it a syndrome. We'll just go back and start over.

[SAM *and* SARA *kiss and stay connected for a moment. Then they pull apart as time begins to move backward.*]

   We'll just go back and start over. So let's just say I'm having those problems now, and we'll pretend I never *called* it a syndrome.

[STEVE *scratches, then grabs the briefcase and walks backward toward the door.*]

OK.

[*A beat.*]

Can't you just cover me? My doctor down here sent the materials to the claims person, like, a week ago. I don't *know* what caused it. [*Into apartment*] Honey? Honey? [*Into phone*] Multiple Chemical Sensitivity. Listen, M-C-S is a recognized condition.

[SAM *kisses* SARA.]

SARA: Yeah.

[*A moment passes.*]

SAM [*half-scared*]: Do you feel that?

[*A moment passes.*]

Amen.

SARA: Amen.

SAM: Your sign to us, in story, of your endless and ever-present love.

SARA: Your sign to us, in story, of your endless and ever-present love.

SAM: I pray this prayer in the name of Jesus . . .

SARA: I pray this prayer in the name of Jesus . . .

SAM: And together we'll start all over.

STEVE: Look, I've been back and forth with you people about this . . .

SARA: And together we'll start all over.

[STEVE *exits backward out the door. A moment passes. Time moves forward.*]

SARA: And together we'll start all over.

[STEVE *enters from outside, carrying his briefcase and talking on his cell phone. He scratches when he can. He looks unhealthy.*]

STEVE: Look, I've been back and forth with you people about this . . .

SAM: And together we'll start all over.

SARA: I pray this prayer in the name of Jesus . . .

SAM: I pray this prayer in the name of Jesus . . .

SARA: Your sign to us, in story, of your endless and ever-present love.

SAM: Your sign to us, in story, of your endless and ever-present love.

SARA: Amen.

SAM: Amen.

[SAM *and* SARA *both become aware of a feeling—in them, around them.*]

[*Half-scared*] Do you feel that?

[*A moment passes.*]

SARA: Yeah.

STEVE: Listen, M-C-S is a recognized condition. Multiple Chemical Sensitivity. [*Into apartment*] Honey? Honey? [*Into phone*] I don't *know* what caused it. My doctor down here sent the materials to the claims person, like, a week ago. Can't you just cover me?

[*A beat.*]

OK.

[STEVE *sets down the briefcase and bag so he can scratch.*]

So let's just say I'm having those problems now, and we'll pretend I never *called* it a syndrome. We'll just go back and start over.

[SAM *and* SARA *kiss and stay connected.*]

Please. Can't you just tell me I'm covered? I'm not asking to be better, I just want to be covered. I just want—

[*A beat.*]

Hey—hey—can you hang on a second, please, I just have to take this call, I'll be right back.

[STEVE *hits a button on the phone and scratches furiously as he talks.*]

Gary, yeah, thanks for calling me back, they just backed out! The bank! Why do you think, Gary, because we haven't paid them anything! Just now, I just got the call from their lawyers! Yeah! They're suing me for fraud and breach of contract! Because I'm the one whose name is on the purchase agreement! I brought my wife down here, Gary! I closed a successful business and brought my wife and ten guys down here, I brought my whole life down here! Gary—no, Gary, don't tell me Mr. Himmelman's gonna wire the money tomorrow, because you always say that and then he doesn't—no, you say that, Gary, but then it doesn't come—Gary, listen to me, can I please just talk to Mr. Himmelman? Please? Can I talk to Mr. Himmelman?

[*A beat.*]

Is there even really a Mr. Himmelman? I mean, have you ever actually seen him face-to-face? Well, when you do, would you please ask him why he's doing this to me, Gary? Why is Mr. Himmelman doing this to me?

[*A moment passes.* SAM *and* SARA *are still kissing.* STEVE *stands up—*]

GOD DAMN IT!

[*—and smashes his phone into pieces with his foot.*]

SCENE 6

[*It's very late at night.* SARA *is sitting on the floor, despondent.* SAM *is at the table, looking at his three photos. A moment passes. Then* STEVE *enters from the bedroom door in white underwear.* STEVE *itches so much he can't even scratch anymore. It's like he's quietly vibrating with anxiety. Everyone is heartbroken and haunted. The dialogue in this scene is generously striped with silences.*]

STEVE: Honey?

SARA: Yeah?

STEVE: Are you alright?

SARA: Yeah.

STEVE: What's the matter?

SARA: Nothing.

STEVE: It's three thirty.

SARA: I can't sleep.

STEVE: Come to bed.

SARA: I will. In a while.

STEVE: Is something wrong?

SARA: No. I just can't sleep.

STEVE: OK.

[STEVE *exits into the bedroom. And then he enters again.*]

Sara.

SARA: What?

STEVE: This itching is driving me crazy.

SARA: I know. I'm sorry.

[*A moment passes.*]

STEVE: Did you ever have fleas, growing up?

SARA: No.

STEVE: I got fleas once. When I was in third grade. I feel like I've got fleas. A million little microscopic electric fleas. Under my skin.

[*A moment passes.* STEVE *talks, periodically waiting for responses from* SARA, *which don't come.*]

I got a call from the bank today. They're selling the hotel to somebody else. I guess they'd been having conversations with other potential buyers ever since the money didn't come. So it's all probably for the best, because if they were talking to other potential buyers without telling me when I had already signed a purchase agreement, then do I really want to be in business with them anyway? I don't think so. Everybody's so foul.

[*A moment passes.* SAM *lights a candle on the table.*]

Sara?

SARA: What?

STEVE: Wouldja look at me? Please?

[SARA *looks at him.*]

SARA: What?

STEVE: Let's go back to Minnesota. [*A flat joke*] I don't like Florida anymore.

[*A beat.*]

Seriously, though, whaddaya say? Let's go back. You want to, too, don't you? Let's go back.

[*A moment passes. During the following,* SAM *burns the three photographs.*]

SARA: I don't know if we can.

STEVE: What does that mean?

SARA: Just what I said, I don't know if we can. I'm sorry.

STEVE: Sorry for what?

SARA: For not knowing.

[STEVE *moves closer to her.*]

STEVE: Come on. Let's go back home and start the business up again. Just the renovations, or maybe even just general contracting, you know, to get started. We'll get back to the bread-and-butter of the business and we'll build it that way. Seed-harvest, right? You can run the office and I'll get the jobs. We could go back to church.

[*A beat.*]

    Let's go back.

[*A moment passes.*]

SARA: I don't think we can, Steve.

STEVE: Sara—

SARA: I really don't think we can.

[*With painful steps,* STEVE *moves closer to* SARA. *Then*—]

STEVE: Sara, I know this might not seem like the ideal time to bring it up, and please don't take this wrong . . . but Ephesians 5:22 does say, "Wives, submit to your husbands as to the Lord."

[*A beat.*]

    Colossians 3:18 says pretty much the same thing.

SARA: Steve—

STEVE: It's kind of a major biblical principle. So I would just ask you to take that into consideration as you weigh your options right now.

SARA [*more firmly*]: Steve.

[*Beat.*]

STEVE: Yeah?

[*A long beat.*]

SARA: I don't think we should be married anymore.

SCENE 7

[*It's late the next morning.* SARA *and* SAM *are on the sofa.* STEVE *is sitting between them.* STEVE *opens a Cabela's bag and removes a box from it. He opens the box and takes out a gun and several boxes of bullets. He opens one of the boxes and loads the gun with one bullet. He snaps the cylinder into place, spins the cylinder, and puts it to his head. He cocks it. He shuts his eyes.*]

SAM: I feel like I could look at you forever.

[STEVE *fires. Click.*]

SARA: Me too.

[STEVE *loads a second bullet into the gun, snaps it shut, spins the cylinder, puts it to his head.*]

SAM: You should go back home.

SARA: I don't want to.

[STEVE *fires. Click.*]

SAM: OK.

[STEVE *puts a third bullet in, shuts his eyes, and tries again—fires. Click. He opens his eyes. He puts three more bullets in the gun, rises, and exits out the door. Beat. Then there is a knock at the door.*]

SARA: That's him.

SAM: How do you know?

STEVE [*offstage, through the door*]: Sam!

[*More knocks.*]

> [*Offstage, through the door*] Sam, it's Steve, I just wanna talk. Can we talk a second? I just wanna talk. I know you're both in there.

[SARA *gives* SAM *a worried look.*]

SAM: It's gonna be OK.

[SAM *gets up and opens the door.* STEVE *is standing there.*]

STEVE: Hi.

SAM: Hi.

STEVE: Can I come in a second?

SAM: Sure.

[STEVE *enters and goes to* SARA. *He's tense but reasonable.*]

STEVE: Sara.

SARA: Steve—

STEVE: I know you're not happy. I know I've made—

SARA: I don't want to—

STEVE: Let me finish! I know I've made mistakes.

[STEVE *looks at* SAM *and then back to* SARA.]

> I would lay them all out for you, one by one, but in my opinion, there are still some things that are between a husband and wife, and we're still husband and wife, and, so, we'll, uh, I'll lay them out for you at a later date. The point is, Sara: please come out of here with me right now and we'll figure this out. Please. Come with me right now, we'll go back to our apartment where we live as husband and wife and we'll figure this out.

SARA: No.

STEVE: Why? Because you're in love with this guy? This guy with . . . with no face?

SARA: Steve, don't be like that.

STEVE: I mean, just look at the situation objectively, Sara, come on, the fact that you have feelings for him must have more to do with you being unhappy than it does with him. [*Including* SAM] I'm just saying, objectively.

SAM: Shut up.

STEVE: No—

SAM: Yeah, it's not, you can't talk to me or her that way—

STEVE: No, *you* can't turn my wife against me and tell me to SHUT UP!

SARA: He didn't turn me against you, Steve—

STEVE: Then who did?

[*All this time,* KARL *moves among them, unseen.*]

SARA: No one! I'm not against you. I just don't want to be with you anymore.

SAM: Steve. Look.

STEVE: Don't talk to me.

SAM: Listen. I don't go through my life trying to hurt people. I don't have a, you know, I don't have a plan.

STEVE: No, I *know* you don't have a plan, you don't have *anything*—

SAM: Listen to me! I acknowledge your right to take your wife back home with you, if you want—

STEVE: Oh, well, thank you very much, Mr. High and Mighty—

SAM:—and if *she* wants—but, uh, I just want you to know: she, uh . . . she is a sign to me: she's a message that, uh . . . that I'm not dead. That it's not a mistake that I'm still alive. That life is maybe about more than I thought it was. She saved me. And I don't know how to say no to that.

STEVE: You're calling this filthy, lying . . . thing that you've done an act of God?

SARA: Steve, we haven't DONE anything!

STEVE: You've broken my heart, Sara! That's what you've done! You've broken my heart! [*To* SAM] This isn't God.

SAM: I never said it was "God" . . .

STEVE: No, but that's what you mean, you mean God sent her to you and He saved you—

SAM: No, I'm saying, that's how it feels!

STEVE: No way! No way! No way!

[*A beat.*]

No way!

[*Beat.*]

No way did I sit in a Bible Study of Romans seven years ago and see the prettiest girl I'd ever seen in my life. No way did I wait five months to ask her out, praying every night about it, because I didn't feel like I could ever, like I could ever be good enough for her. No way did I ask her out to dinner and she said yes. No way did we quit smoking together. No way did we get married. No way did we go to her father's funeral, and then to my father's funeral in the same month. No way did I take her to the emergency room one night and watch her almost die and pray on my knees in a broom closet that she would live, and she did. No way did we make love. Ever. No way was I legally promised fourteen million dollars to purchase hotels. No way did we move down here. No way did everything, everything go wrong. No way did I buy a gun—

[STEVE *pulls out a gun but doesn't aim it.* SAM *and* SARA *recoil.*]

—and keep it hidden in my sock drawer for week after week without you finding it! No way did I try to kill myself with it three times and fail, only to stand here and lose my wife to a man with no face.

[STEVE *aims the gun at* SAM's *face.*]

And no faith.

[STEVE *cocks the gun.*]

No way. No way does God do that to a person. No way.

[*There is a knock at the door.*]

You expecting somebody?

SAM: No.

STEVE: Maybe there's some other woman in the complex you're bewitching with your good looks and space talk . . . ?

SARA: Steve!

[*There are more knocks at the door.*]

KARL [*offstage*]: Hello!?

STEVE [*to* SAM]: Don't move. Don't say a word. And don't move.

[*A moment passes. Then a key turns in the door, and it opens and* KARL *walks in with his sprayer.*]

KARL [*to* SAM]: Oh. Hey there.

STEVE: Shut the door!

KARL [*to* SAM]: Sorry I let myself in, the girl in the office gives me the keys now to save you folks the trouble—

STEVE [*aiming at* KARL]: Shut the door, shut the door!

KARL: OK, OK, I shut the door!

[KARL *shuts the door.*]

STEVE: What are you doing here?

KARL: Spraying for the little guys.

[*A moment passes.*]

I see you got your gun.

STEVE: Yeah.

KARL: Welcome to Florida.

[*A tense moment passes.* KARL *exchanges a look with* SAM *and* SARA *and then returns his focus to* STEVE.]

Jesus Freak . . .

STEVE: What?

[KARL *picks up his spray can.*]

What are you doing?

KARL: I told you, I'm spraying for the little guys . . .

[KARL *starts moving through the room, spraying.*]

. . . but listen to me, I got something to tell you.

[STEVE *still has the gun raised but watches with bafflement as* KARL *disregards him and moves through the space.*]

STEVE: What?

KARL: My wife died from the cancer.

[KARL *passes near* SARA.]

SARA: I'm sorry.

KARL: S'okay, it's not your fault. [*To* STEVE] But I went to Miami to be with her family last week for the service, you know. And after the service at the crematorium, I go to the cemetery. We lay her in the ground. But after we lay her in the ground, I am walking back to the car when there is a woman across the little lane there, by the bench, and she walk past me on her way to the gate. And as she pass me, I look—and I think—this is not possible.

SARA: Rachel . . . ?

KARL: Yah! [*To* SAM] S'okay if I go in the bedroom?

SAM: Yeah. Sure.

KARL: I always ask.

[KARL *exits into the bedroom but keeps talking.*]

So I say, "Rachel, is that you?" And Jesus Freak, she looked at me. She looked at me with those eyes.

[*A moment passes and* KARL *comes back into the doorway.*]

So we go have coffee at Starbucks.

[KARL *now goes to* STEVE, *whose hand is trembling on his gun.*]

And while we're sitting there at the Starbucks, I tell her how sorry I am for what happened, you know? How I told the Nazis where she was hiding and how I did the things they made me do. And I said, "I was scared, Rachel, I'm sorry. I didn't know what to do, I was a young boy, I didn't know how to be, you know, I didn't know how to be brave enough at that time; and maybe I'll never know how to be that brave, I don't know, all I know is I'm sorry." And you know what she says to me?

STEVE: What?

KARL: Jesus Freak, she says to me the sweetest words I have ever heard in my life. My dear departed wife, I love her dearly, but I never heard this so big in my heart, she says to me: "I understand."

[*A moment passes.*]

"I understand."

[*A beat.*]

After what I did to her, she says that to *me*.

[*A moment passes.*]

So this is what I want to say to you, Jesus Freak. I don't know if there is any Jesus. I don't know if there is any God. But there is *something*. I know this now. There is something in the world that *waits*. There is something in the world that *waits*—and then sometimes it come backs—[*correcting himself*]—sometimes it comes back for us.

[*As* KARL *looks at* STEVE, *the "Do you feel that?" sound starts.*]

Do you understand?

[*A moment passes.*]

STEVE: Yeah.

[STEVE *slowly lowers the gun completely.*]

Yeah. I understand.

KARL: Good. That's good.

[KARL *pulls an official-looking paper form from his back pocket and goes to* SAM. *Note: the "Do you feel that?" sound continues.*]

[*To* SAM] You're feeling better now, huh?

SAM: Thanks.

[KARL *hands* SAM *the form.*]

What's this?

KARL: S'a sad story. We start using organic pesticide now, because, uh, some people have had bad reaction to the Dursban.

[STEVE, SARA, *and* SAM *all register this key information.*]

Not me, you know, fifty years I've been working with the stuff— every morning, with the pushups and squats—but we make the switch, so, if you sign this, you promise you don't sue us, we give you a coupon.

SAM: For what?

KARL: A hang gliding lesson.

STEVE: A hang gliding lesson . . . ?

KARL: Yah, because the owner of the company, you know, he's a hang glider.

[KARL *turns to* STEVE.]

I'll leave one for you too.

[KARL *picks up his sprayer, goes to the door, opens it, and looks at* STEVE *until he feels the situation is under control. Then he says . . .*]

Bye.

[*. . . and exits. A moment passes.* SAM *and* SARA *exchange a look about the gracious mystery of the Rachel story.*]

SARA [*with awe, moved*]: Rachel.

[*A moment passes.*]

Praise God.

[*A long moment passes.*]

STEVE: God. One night I went out under the stars. The stars? Because a lot of people had, what, told me something? Because some people had told me something, I went outside and looked up at the stars. I spoke to them like you would to a person, and they talked back. I would give anything, anything, to forget they did, but I can't. I talked to the stars and they talked back and something shot through me, it did, down through the top of my head like an upside-down fountain and I was filled for the first time with a sense of love. "Universal love." And so I did what any poor, stupid, helpless human being would do. I changed everything. I reorganized my entire life around this "universal love" that I thought I saw, that I thought I felt. It felt like the most perfection and beauty I'd ever felt in my life, and this is how it ends up?

[STEVE *abruptly raises the gun and aims at* SAM.]

SARA: Don't.

STEVE: *Just tell me this is how it ends up!!*

SARA: It doesn't have to!

STEVE: It feels like it does, though, doesn't it? It feels like it does!

SARA: Please, Steve, just tell me what you want—

STEVE: I want to go back, Sara! Remember the little monkeys? I want to go back.

SARA: We can't.

[STEVE *cocks the gun.*]

SAM: Don't. Please. Don't.

[STEVE *holds it there, aimed at* SAM, *shaking with uncertainty and fear, long enough that we're no longer sure what's going to happen next.*]